[CODING YOUR PASSION™]

USING COMPUTER SCIENCE IN HEALTH CARE CAREERS

DON RAUF

Rosen YA™
New York

Published in 2019 by The Rosen Publishing Group, Inc.
29 East 21st Street, New York, NY 10010

First Edition

Library of Congress Cataloging-in-Publication Data

Names: Rauf, Don, author.
Title: Using computer science in health care careers / Don Rauf.
Description: First edition. | New York : Rosen YA, 2019. | Series: Coding your passion | Audience: Grades 7–12. | Includes bibliographical references and index.
Identifiers: LCCN 2018013455 | ISBN 9781508183976 (library bound) | ISBN 9781508183969 (paperback)
Subjects: LCSH: Medical informatics—Vocational guidance—Juvenile literature. | Medical technology—Vocational guidance—Juvenile literature.
Classification: LCC R858 .R38 2019 | DDC 610.285—dc23
LC record available at https://lccn.loc.gov/2018013455

Manufactured in the United States of America

CONTENTS

INTRODUCTION

For those interested in health care careers, one of the biggest changes has been the need to adapt and learn about advances in computer technology. Digital technology continues to drive innovation and growth in the business of health and well-being.

Health care is a people-oriented field—all those who pursue careers in this area are ultimately concerned about human welfare. Nurses, doctors, and other health care providers interact with patients in a one-on-one way. Although the jobs involve this personal exchange, technology has increasingly played a role in health care, improving the health of patients and making the lives of care providers easier. To bring this technology to life requires the skills of computer programmers, software developers, and coders.

The health care industry has been a leader in terms of job creation, and those who have at least some knowledge of programming and coding may find they are more desirable in the job market. Programming and coding are valuable skills, which cut across a variety of disciplines.

The US Bureau of Labor Statistics (BLS) reports that the future is bright for those interested in information technology and health. Across the board, job growth is anticipated in the field well into the next decade, especially as the world's aging population continues to live longer.

Through medical imaging technologies such as computed tomography (CT), magnetic resonance

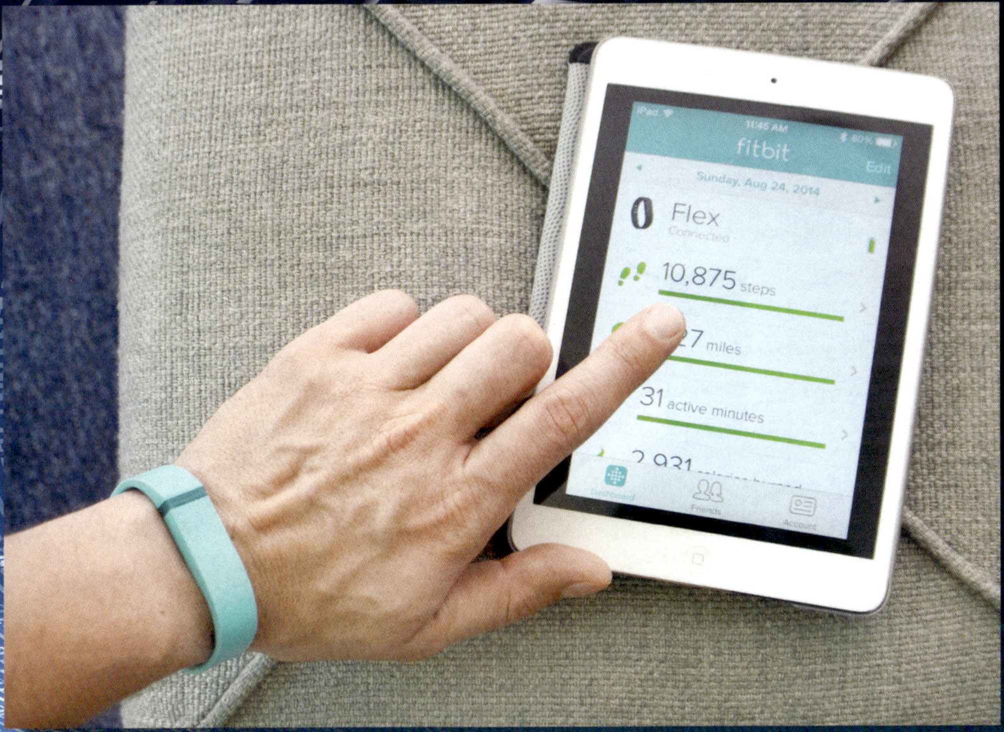

Computer technology is the driving force behind many areas of health care, from robot-assisted surgery to wearable electronics that monitor health, such as the Fitbit Flex, pictured here.

imaging (MRI), and X-ray, health care professionals can map out details in a human body to accurately diagnose problems and carefully visualize what procedures can help. Using robotics, surgeons can perform delicate heart operations with more precision. Advances have made it possible for doctors to control scalpel-wielding robots and operate on people from afar. The robotic equipment typically responds as commanded because of the computer programming that controls it.

On a smaller level, tech-savvy individuals have been developing phone apps that help patients monitor health. "We believe consumer health technologies—apps, wearables, self-diagnosis tools—have the potential to strengthen the patient-physician connection and improve health outcomes," says Dr. Glen Stream, chairman, Family Medicine for America's Health.

Behind the scenes, computer programming is also at work in the labs. Medical labs rely on technology for analyzing blood, tissue, urine, and other bodily samples. Researchers also make sense of huge amounts of data with the help of computer software. Pharmaceutical companies depend on tech professionals as well to crunch the numbers from medical studies so results can be interpreted.

Because patients generate a continual flood of paperwork, software has helped to organize, store, and access the data. When it comes to health care services delivery, management, and planning, computers are now a key part of the process.

Employers wanting tech-savvy hires include hospitals, pharmaceutical firms, biotech companies, universities, and data management services. Learning to code doesn't have to be an overwhelming chore. Though courses can be taken on a full-time basis, there are many part-time learning options as well as online classes that let you master skills at your own speed. No matter what jobs in the medical field interest you, computer skills can boost your career and widen your prospects.

CHAPTER ONE

CALLING ALL CODERS

Neurosurgeon Pieter Kubben is a firm believer in learning how to code. In fact, he thinks all physicians should learn the skill because it not only can help lift their careers but it can also open the door to health care solutions that help both patients and practitioners.

Although becoming a professional programmer may take at least three to four years of study, Kubben says that amateurs can get a grasp on the basics in a short amount of time. "It is not hard at all to buy/download a book on computer programming, or watch an online video tutorial, and get some hands-on experience," he wrote in an article titled "Why Physicians Might Want to Learn Computer Programming," published in *Surgical Neurology International.*

No matter what segment of the health care field you explore, computer programmers are at work. Although the US Bureau of Labor Statistics reports that opportunities for programmers may decline slightly by 2026, the demand for them is strong and wages are high. Software developers, the creative

Programmers and software developers are in high demand, so employment opportunities are plentiful and the jobs typically pay very well.

minds who make applications, are expected to see high job growth.

THE FUNDAMENTALS

Some may think programming requires immense brainpower and their minds will short-circuit if they even attempt to learn the skill. The fact is, you don't have to be a math whiz or computer genius to master some programming basics. Curiosity, logical thinking, and an inclination toward problem solving

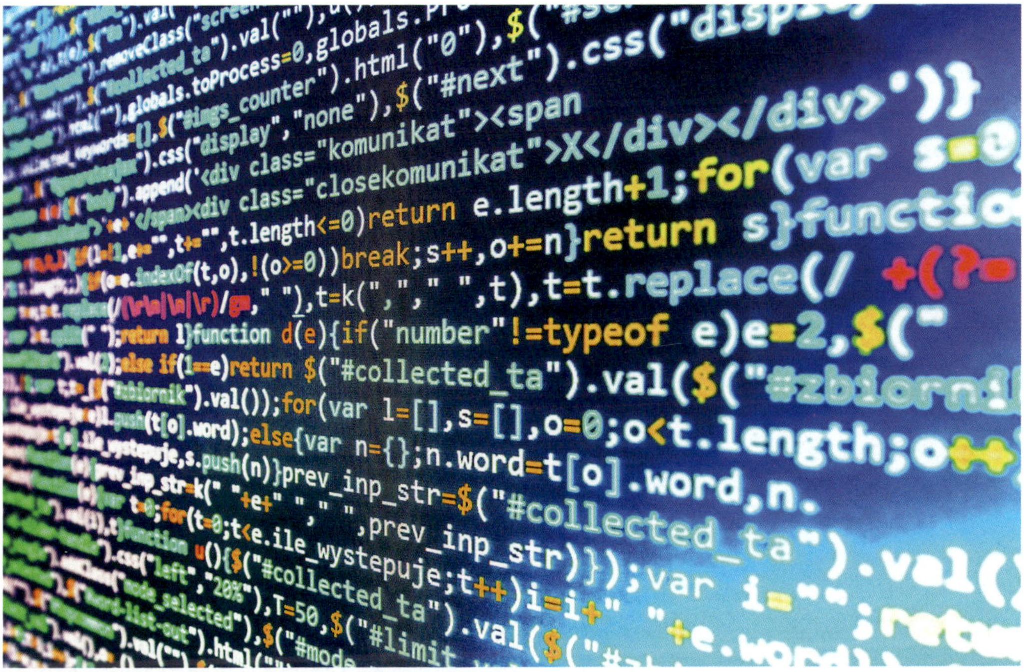

Learning to code is like learning a foreign language. At first, it may all look impossible to understand, but with practice and time, a person can become fluent.

are key. After all, people write code to solve problems. The other essential ingredient is patience because learning to code means learning a new language—or more than one. Like learning any foreign language, it takes constant practice to become fluent.

Code writing, or programming, is the process of creating a set of instructions that tell a computer how to perform a certain task. When you put information into a computer, it needs to know what to do with it. Various languages are used in programming, such as Java, C++, C, Python, and SQL. You can play with programming languages on your personal computer, but typically you have to first download a programming language platform, which will allow you to configure the language for use on your system.

Programmers put code together to complete software. The process involves a lot of trial and error—testing, finding the bugs, and correcting those problems.

Though there can be a certain amount of repetitiveness in writing code, it is a tool that can lead to some very creative solutions. Donald Knuth, a pioneer in the field and author of *The Art of Computer Programming*, wrote, "Computer programming is an art, because it applies accumulated knowledge to the world, because it requires skill and ingenuity, and especially because it produces objects of beauty."

EDUCATE YOURSELF

For those who want to pursue a career that relies heavily on programming, a higher-education degree may be necessary. Many employers want to see at least an associate's or bachelor's degree in computer science, mathematics, or information systems, according to the Bureau of Labor Statistics. A graduate degree such as a master's or higher can help to learn advance concepts and applications. Standard courses include program design, systems analysis, computer architecture, and database management. Depending on your interest in health care, you can find courses that meet your specific needs. For instance, colleges provide coursework in health administration, medical billing, and health informatics.

ONLINE OPTIONS

There are many disciplines in coding. Depending on the exact job, a health care professional may want to explore some of the online courses listed here and then decide which to study.

- Codecademy. Since 2011, Codecademy has provided free interactive coding classes for different programming languages, including Java. The site charges for some additional services.
- Khan Academy. This organization provides several step-by-step video tutorials.
- LearnJavaOnline.org. This free interactive tutorial is designed for all levels of programmers—from absolute beginners to the more experienced.
- MIT Open Courseware. MIT offer a series of free online classes for all levels, from beginners to computer whizzes. It's Introduction to Computer Science course is geared toward students with zero or minimal programming experience.
- Udemy. Started in 2009, Udemy has offered more than 65,000 online courses. Hundreds of thousands of students have taken its Java Tutorial for Complete Beginners, which is designed for those who don't have prior programming knowledge.

(continued on the next page)

(continued from the previoust page)

- **YouthDigital.com. This resource offers online tech courses that teach kids ages eight to fourteen how to code, design, develop, and animate.**

Certificate programs are also available that let an individual complete short-term coursework and then pass a test demonstrating that he or she has mastered a particular computer language or skill.

There are many possible educational paths to gaining programming skills, such as taking online classes or completing college courses that provide internships working alongside seasoned professionals.

Even some experience in coding can help a person become a better problem solver and interact with more experienced computer experts.

The best way to get a grasp on coding in real life is to see it in action. Internships often give students a firsthand look at what a programmer does. Through internships, students generally work for a company or organization and see what a job is like on a day-to-day basis while still earning class credit. A mentor (an older, more experienced individual) can also give advice and insight into an occupation.

CHAPTER TWO

CONTROLLING THE DATA AVALANCHE

According to research organization the Ponemon Institute, the health care industry produces approximately 30 percent of the world's stored data. An article in the *New England Medical Journal* noted that typically an individual generates about 80 megabytes annually in imaging and electronic medical record (EMR) data. All information must be carefully stored so it can be easily accessed by patients and doctors. Managing the mountains of data has become a sophisticated science. Database administrators depend on distinct software to organize and store data.

THE WORLD OF HEALTH CARE INFORMATICS

The science and practice of collecting health care information, and then storing it so it can be used later by a patient's different health care providers, is called

Using the latest technology, health care providers can quickly access patient medical histories, including previous treatments and diagnoses, via handheld devices, such as tablet computers.

health care informatics. Informatics can apply to research as well.

In the days of old, a patient's health history was recorded on paper and stored in file cabinets. Today, that data goes into an electronic health record (EHR). Starting in 2014, federal law required that all medical records in the United States be converted into an electronic format. Doctors and nurses record their observations in the electronic system. With the push of a button, authorized users can view medical and treatment histories—diagnoses, suggested treatments, medications, dates of immunizations, allergy history, X-rays, and lab results can all be viewed instantly from doctors' offices, homes, or anywhere a person has computer access. These online records make it easy to monitor patient progress and notify individuals if they are due for a visit or screening.

Software created by the company Medopad, for example, lets doctors see patient records via an iPad, including notes from nurses and other attendants. The Medopad software provides real-time vital signs as well, along with tools to order tests or medications.

The Office of the National Coordinator for Health Information Technology says that computer systems make it possible to share the records with "laboratories, specialists, medical imaging facilities, pharmacies, emergency facilities, and school and workplace clinics." The right software setup can let a doctor order lab tests or prescriptions with just a few clicks. Health records are often integrated with billing systems. Providers must get paid for their services—they track that they have billed patients accordingly and submitted for payment to their medical insurance companies.

A DIFFERENT TYPE OF CODING

The tracking of diagnoses, procedures, and medical services requires specific medical coding. Medical coding is the use of universally accepted numbers and letters that represent these items. Every treatment has a corresponding code. Coding is key for doctors to get reimbursed, and as you might imagine, there are thousands of these codes. Injuries and illnesses have codes established by the International Classification of Diseases. On the procedure side, actions are classified according to Current Procedure Terminology (CPT). The medical coder makes sure all is properly labeled and sent off to a patient's insurance company in a claim. The coder inputs all the info via specific computer software.

The software allows the code to submit the claim to the insurance company, which comes back the doctor's office with an amount it will cover for the service. Then the coder figures out how much of the bill the patient owes after subtracting how much the insurance company will cover. Software generates a financial report covering how much is paid and how much is owed.

In the world of medical record keeping, every diagnosis, procedure, and service gets a universal code of letters and numbers. This type of coding helps with billing and insurance claims.

The computer programmer builds and maintains the digital infrastructure to support and manipulate all this information. Software programs such as Epic, Centricity, AdvancedMD, Flash Code, Eclipse, and others provide fields where coders enter the correct procedure and diagnosis codes.

The latest US Bureau of Labor Statistics reports that positions for health informatics technicians are expected to grow 15 percent between 2014 and 2024. Medical records and health information technician opportunities are expected to grow 13 percent between 2016 and 2026. Many employers prefer to hire those with certification, such as the Registered Health Information Technician (RHIT) designation, which is offered by the American Health Information Management Association. Some certification training programs can be completed in six to nine months.

NURSES TAKE ON INFORMATICS

Often nurses lack the IT skills to enable them to develop systems, but a growing number of nurses are specializing in informatics, or the science of processing data. The American Nursing Association says that these nurses oversee the integration of data to support decision making by patients and their health care providers. They may devote a bulk of their time to systems development, where they customize or update systems or create a system that is tailored for their needs. To do this, knowledge of programming can help them shape how a health records operation is established.

BETTER CARE THROUGH DATA RESEARCH

Amber Crea, a nurse in the intensive care unit at Harbor View Medical Center in Seattle, said that she and colleagues have been working on a research project based on hospital data to see how paging health care providers may disrupt patient care.

According to Slate.com, a 2016 survey found that 85 percent of hospitals still rely on pagers (small electronic devices that receive messages) to contact doctors quickly. Crea and her collaborators thought that paging may be interrupting doctors from taking care of others.

Using computer software and the hospital's data collection, they pulled data from tens of thousands of pages. They compared the times of the pages to times when patients were admitted into intensive care. They found that many of the pages were happening during admissions or overnight when there are fewer providers (doctors)—indicating that pages would be interrupting at important times for patient care.

Crea and her team will now look at solutions—for example, identifying situations that nurses can manage themselves rather than paging doctors, and educating nurses and patients on paging practices with the goal of reducing the number of avoidable pages.

"Learning to code puts you in the driver's seat, and allows you to actively shape the future of nursing informatics," wrote Allen McClean in the *Canadian Journal of Nursing Informatics*. He wrote that computational thinking teaches how to tackle large problems by breaking them down into sequences of smaller, more manageable problems—and that can help any nurse.

Kathryn Yuh studied to be a nurse and later learned programming. On the Code Fellows website, she says that both fields require you to work collaboratively as a valuable and reliable team member, and you must also know how to work cooperatively and effectively under high-stress scenarios, as well as demonstrate a solid work ethic on a day-to-day basis.

ESSENTIAL TRAINING REQUIRED

Health care professionals get a firsthand look at the problems that data management programs need to handle. They understand the workflow and can talk to other professionals to understand how systems can be improved. Adelphi University, which offers courses in health informatics, stresses that professionals need to hone their analytical skills to evaluate processes and weigh solutions. Programming knowledge of Java, C, Python, and SQL are useful for working with many electronic health records and health databases.

Those who delve deep into coding learn about data structure, which can get very complex. Patients are very sensitive about keeping their records private and secure, so programmers in this area learn about telecommunications security, security management practices, and security architecture. The coding pros write software that protects against cyber attacks and safety breaches.

There are other careers in health informatics, too. Chief medical information officers are typically in charge of the design, implementation, and use of health informatics technology within an organization. A director of clinical informatics promotes the understanding and application of that technology in the health care setting. Computer and information systems managers who coordinate computer-related

Nurses and other health care professionals who have some programming skills can gain a better understanding of how information management works and get a leg up in their careers.

activities for an organization can expect opportunities to rise over the next ten years.

SIFTING THROUGH THE DATA

All the data collected on patients in a hospital or other organization may reveal helpful trends. A clinical data analyst will comb through the mountains of figures and facts and identify and interpret patterns and details. An article on the website HealthCatalyst reports hospitals that hire data analysts have the potential to save millions of dollars. One hospital was looking at making a major investment in expanding its emergency room department because it was getting overloaded. When a data analyst used software to examine various facts about the hospital, he found that a high number of patients with chest pain were going to the emergency room between 5 p.m. and 10 p.m. The analyst discovered that the hospital's separate cardiac clinic closed at 5 p.m. The solution was to keep the cardiac clinic open longer. Using the right software, the data analyst could compare costs of investing in expanding the emergency room versus extending cardiac clinic hours.

CHAPTER THREE

KEEPING AN ELECTRONIC EYE ON HEALTH

Before computers and technology swept through hospitals and offices of care providers, doctors would monitor patients the old-fashioned way—a stethoscope to listen to the heart, lungs, and other inner workings of the body; fingers on the wrist to check the heartbeat; and a tongue depressor to examine the mouth and throat. Although health care providers still use some simple hands-on methods to assess patients, computerized devices have taken monitoring and testing individuals to a whole new level.

Take a look along the bedside of any patient in the hospital and you'll see a variety of monitors gathering and measuring vital signs. Powered by microprocessors, these machines quickly identify changes and complications in the patient's condition. These monitors can gauge several different vital signs, showing them on the screen, and sounding

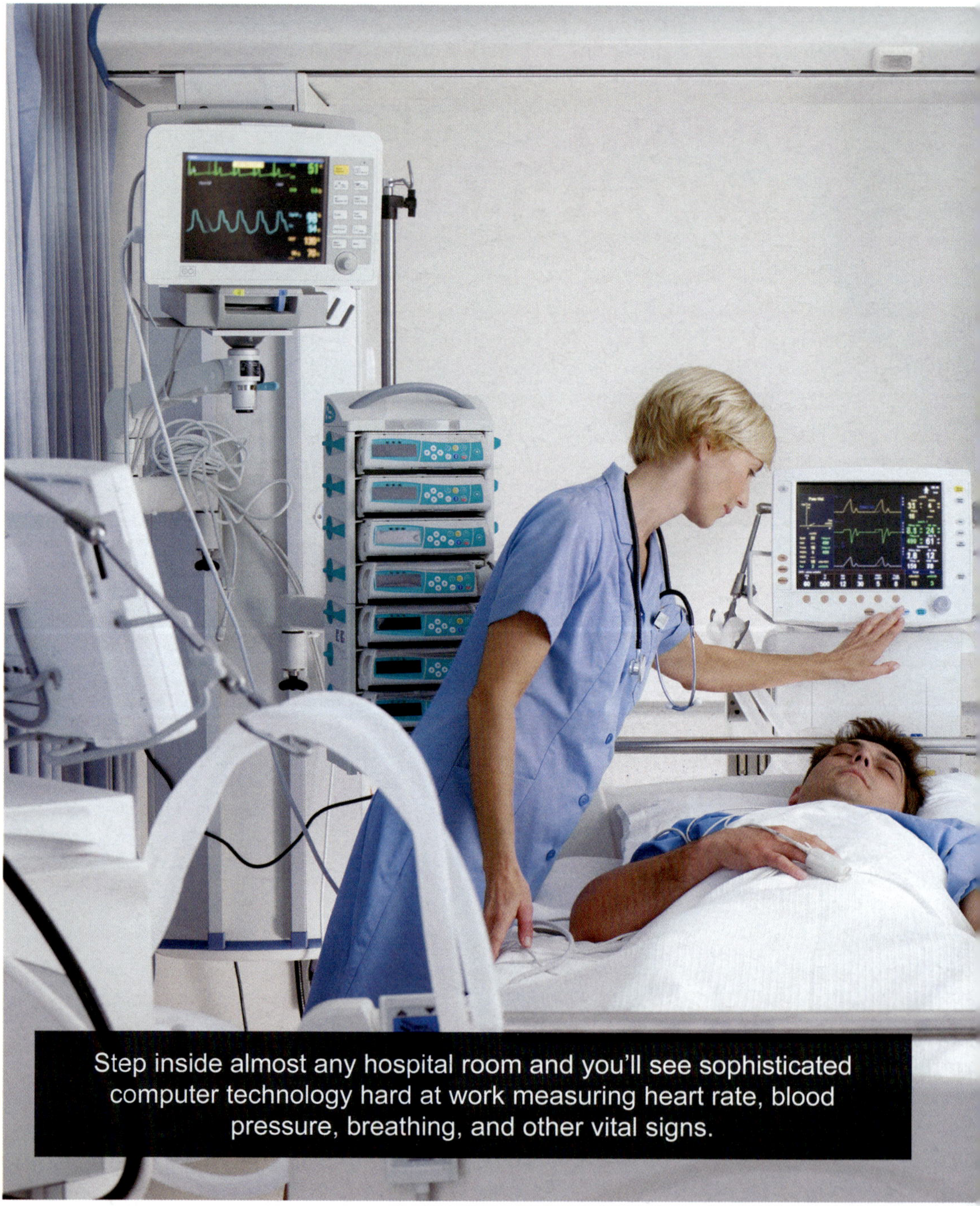

Step inside almost any hospital room and you'll see sophisticated computer technology hard at work measuring heart rate, blood pressure, breathing, and other vital signs.

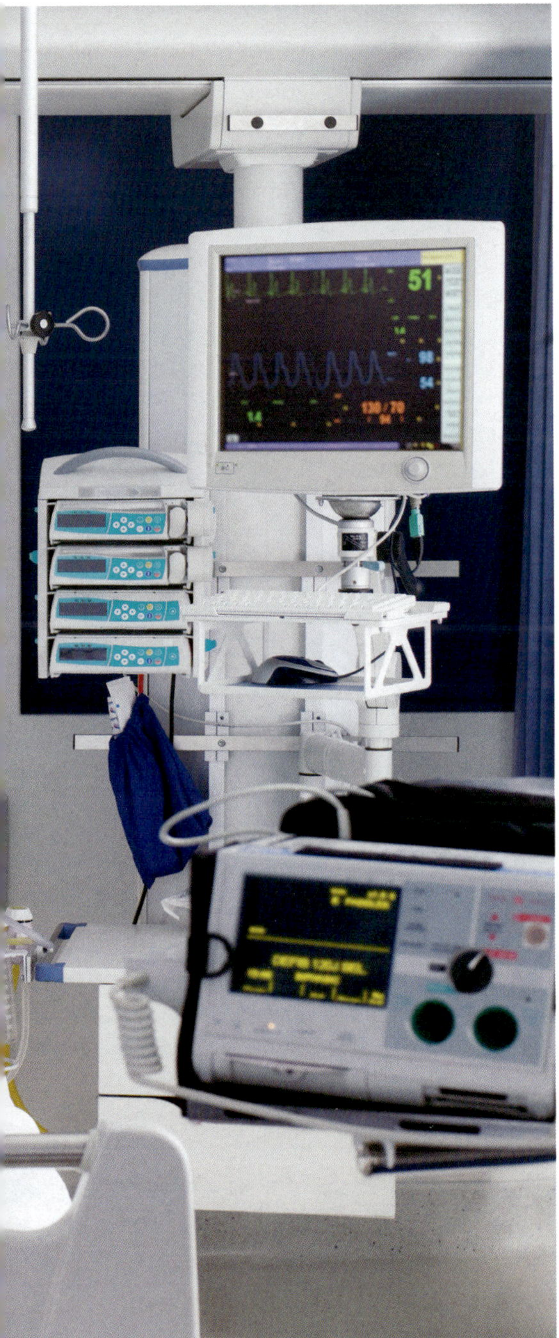

the alarm to inform the care team if something is amiss.

Small sensors attached to the body deliver information to the monitors, which display the data on a screen. Body temperature, heart rate, blood pressure, respiration (rate of breathing), and oxygenation (blood oxygen levels) are all displayed and being updated continually. Sometimes patients will be attached to electrocardiogram (EKG) machines that record the electrical activity of the heart. Then health care providers can review records of heart rhythms and identify any problems. During surgery, subtle changes in an EKG can signal that there is damage occurring to the organ, which alerts a surgeon to pause or stop to find out what the problem is.

Data from monitors feed into centralized computer systems where information can be viewed, recorded, and stored in one main location. In situations in which a critically ill patient needs to be rushed through the hospital, a lightweight device may be required to keep track of vital signs. Providers can even check on patient vital signs via their mobile devices and respond to situations remotely.

CODING MACHINES TO SAVE LIVES

Some of the leaders in patient monitoring systems are Philips Healthcare, Medtronic, Honeywell, Bosch Healthcare Solutions, and Biotronik. Software programmers and developers create the operating functions behind these tools—sometimes they work directly with hospitals and other health care groups to customize the monitoring networks.

Because of the right software and programming, anesthesia used to sedate a patient can be automatically controlled during surgical operations. A computerized system can detect the hypnotic state of a patient at all times and supply the most appropriate doses of anesthesia.

An electrocardiogram informs the doctor about the patient's heart rate and rhythm, changes in blood electrolytes, or thickening of the heart muscle from high blood pressure. Respiration, blood oxygen, and brain activity are all gauged. Brain activity is often measured through electroencephalography (EEG). This evaluates electrical energy being generated in the brain by placing noninvasive electrodes along the scalp.

Specialized software used with CT and MRI scanners can give doctors a detailed view of organs and functions inside the human body.

IMAGING DEPENDS ON PROGRAMMING

Imaging technology has also been immensely helpful to physicians in identifying and diagnosing health problems. X-rays, CT scans, and MRIs let clinicians view inside the human body. MRI technology shows where the programmer's handiwork comes into play.

With MRI software, the inside of the body can be imaged in different layers, called anatomical planes. Together, these "planes" produce 3D images. The MRI software creates an image that can be seen on the computer screen. Powerful magnets inside MRI scanners cause protons in the body to line up. When radio waves are applied, the protons give off a signal that an MRI scanner can read. To carry out these scanning functions and translate the collected data into images, the scanner needs specific software.

Software developers are continually looking for ways to improve the technology—to simplify, make faster, and acquire better images. For example, coders at GE Healthcare created MAGiC (MAGnetic resonance image Compilation) software, which gives doctors more information than standard scanning. With this software, doctors can adjust image contrast after scanning is finished—something that conventional MR does not allow. For a long time, MR imaging of the lungs was difficult until new advances in programming. Software has reduced scan times and simplified taking images of the heart.

EYEAGNOSIS

In 2016, seventeen-year-old Kavya Kopparapu came up with Eyeagnosis, a smartphone app that can screen for diabetic retinopathy, a condition in which

(continued on the next page)

Teenager Kavya Kopparapu combined her loves of health care and computer science to create an app that can detect the eye disease diabetic retinopathy using a phone and a 3D-printed lens.

(continued from the previous page)

high blood sugar can make blood vessels swell and leak. The damage can lead to blindness if not identified and treated soon enough. Kopparapu was inspired to invent the app when her grandfather in India began showing signs of the disease. After she attended a workshop sponsored by the National Center for Women and Information Technology, she got hooked on computer programming. She went home and taught herself C, Python, HTML, and Java. The app works along with a 3D-printed lens that attaches to the phone so a proper image of the eye can be acquired.

To develop her app, Kopparapu turned to sophisticated artificial intelligence (AI). AI is a branch of computer science that aims to use software and computers to perform tasks that usually can be done only with human intelligence. These tasks may involve visual perception or speech recognition. She relied on a form of AI called a convolutional neural network (CNN) that can sift through vast sets of data and look for patterns of similarity.

This type of advanced technology depends on a deep-learning framework that uses languages such as Python and C++. Kopparapu's life goal is to continue to combine her passions for computer science and health care and to inspire other young women to follow her path.

WEARABLE HEALTH TECH

Increasingly, individuals are using wearable devices, such as fitness trackers, to monitor their health as well. These devices require software and computer coding. Several types of wristwatch-style gizmos on the market like Fitbit, UP by Jawbone, Apple's iWatch, and Garmin Vivosport count steps, record sleep patterns, report on calories burned, and display heart rate. Because fitness trackers have become so popular, 4-H (the youth development and mentoring organization) challenged schoolchildren to design and construct a wearable fitness tracker that is both attractive and simple to use as part of its National Youth Science Day. Along with using their programming skills, young people constructed physical circuits and integrated sensors to produce a viable device that could interpret health data.

With smartphones and other mobile devices, apps have been helping people improve their health. An app, which is short for application, is software that can run through a web browser but is often operated on smartphones and tablets. Like wearables, apps can track fitness measures, such as steps walked, heart rate, and more.

CHAPTER FOUR

MEDICAL LAB TECHNOLOGY

Behind the scenes in health care, computer software is an integral part of the day-to-day operation of all medical laboratories. Medical laboratory science (also called clinical laboratory science) has been called the hidden profession that saves lives.

In the lab, out of sight from public view, technicians perform patient medical tests using sophisticated equipment and computer programs. For example, the right computer program can almost instantly tell if a person's protein levels, sugars, and amino acids are normal. Computer programs may assist in determining elements in samples of blood, saliva, tissue, and urine. Getting these results fast can be critical to diagnosing illness and saving lives.

THE FUTURE OF BLOOD TESTING

Before the 1950s, a technician would have to use a microscope to acquire complete blood counts

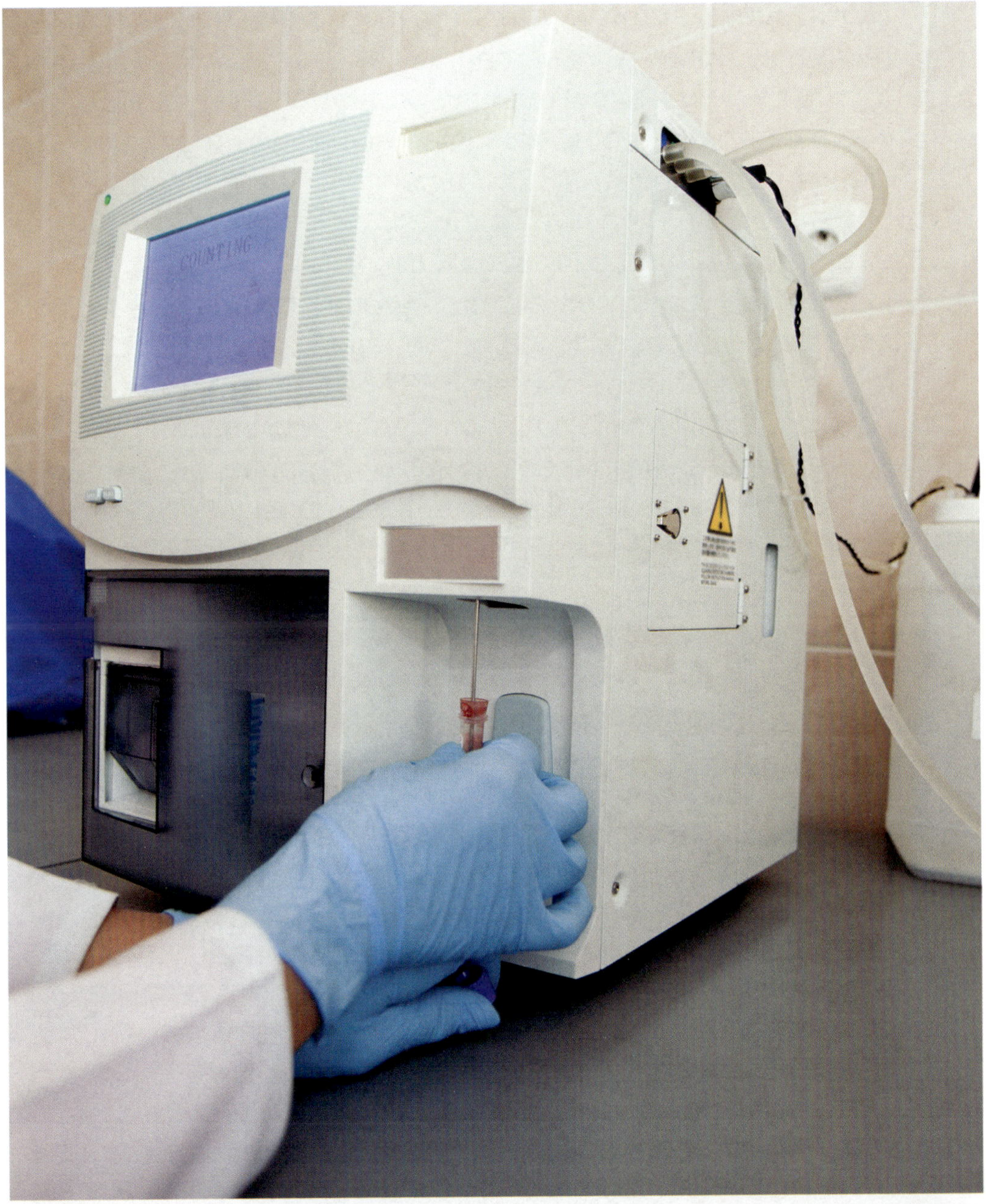

Doctors use blood tests to diagnose disease and determine how well organs are working. Blood-analyzing equipment and software do the job fast and accurately.

(CBC). Today, software does the job via sophisticated hardware. Some devices operate by passing blood through a very narrow opening so that only one cell can pass through at a time. One electrode on either side captures information. A specific arterial blood gas (ABG) test can measure acidity, or pH, and the levels of oxygen (O_2) and carbon dioxide (CO_2).

Over the years, computer programming has advanced the possibilities of lab blood tests. In 2017, researchers at the University of California in Los Angeles working with collaborators at the University of Southern California developed a computer program to detect cancer based on chemical modification of DNA circulating in blood. The program, called

EVEN MICROSCOPES ARE COMPUTERIZED

Microscopes have given scientists the means to discover microorganisms, study the structure of cells, and see the smallest parts of living creatures. Today, medical lab workers may look at samples under a digital microscope, which is a variation of the traditional optical microscope, but this modern viewing device can output and capture images in a computer through special software. By means of software running on a computer, some digital microscopes can output 3D images. Electron microscopes have brought visuals to a molecular level, using a beam of electrons to create an image of the specimen.

Cancer Locator, can detect cancer in blood samples containing low levels of DNA from tumor cells, which reflect early stage disease.

CAPTURING THE RESULTS

Programmers work on software for laboratory information systems (LIS), which record, manage, and store data for clinical laboratories. The LIS tracks and maintains clinical details about a patient's lab history, keeping the information stored in its database for

Using medical equipment and computers, lab technicians may perform tests on tissue, blood, or other bodily samples to help diagnose illness.

future reference. Typically, hospitals and health care providers will want to tap into that information on an LIS to make decisions about patient treatment.

Medical lab work can involve medication testing, reviewing and analyzing data on thousands of compounds that might lead to the development of a life-saving drug. Coders in this area may also work on computer simulations that can help predict the effectiveness of a medication or establish the best course of treatment for a patient.

LAB LABOR NEEDS

All the medical laboratory technology has opened up a range of employment opportunities. According to the Bureau of Labor Statistics, a shortage of laboratory personnel is expected to remain high into the near future. Overall employment of medical laboratory technologists and technicians is projected to grow 13 percent from 2016 to 2026, faster than the average for all occupations.

The BLS says that skills and expertise involving computer software and hardware, electronic equipment, circuit boards, chips, and processors can benefit clinical lab technologists. Many positions require candidates to have some experience with various software programs because these professionals often have to write software or use it to process information and set up functions.

In general, entry-level job candidates must have completed a certificate program (which can last

Computers are crucial for reading and analyzing DNA sequencing (the order of nucleotide bases in a sequence of DNA). This genetic information can help with disease diagnosis and treatment.

one year) or earn a two-year associate's degree in medical laboratory sciences. For those who write software for lab equipment and tests, a knowledge of microbiology, biochemistry, and histology (the study of the microscopic structure of tissues) is required. A coder in this field looks for solutions to improve processes. He or she may dig deeper into courses covering phlebotomy (the practice of drawing blood), hematology (the study of the physiology of blood), urinalysis, viruses, and parasites.

A YOUNG RESEARCHER'S PROGRAMMING SUCCESS

Seung-been "Steven" Lee, a PhD candidate at the University of Washington, loves both medical research and computer science. He has been developing a cutting-edge computer program that correlates a patient's DNA profile with what dose of painkiller is best. He started his academic career majoring in biochemistry as an undergraduate at the University of Washington because he wanted to become a medical doctor. His plans changed course after he took an introductory biology class and started learning about DNA. To pursue his new fascination with DNA, he took an undergraduate research position at a lab studying DNA replication using yeast cells (the same yeast cells used to brew beer). As part of his PhD studies, he took computer science courses.

"I was amazed by what computers can do to solve complex biological questions and health problems," says Lee. "I like computer science because computers do not make mistakes. If a program produces an error, that is because the person who coded the program made a mistake. This feature of computer science is perfect for dealing with health care data because the data tend to be very big and complicated. Humans would easily, and inevitably, make mistakes if they were to handle these kinds of data manually."

Lee also likes working with health care data because he can make a big difference in people's everyday lives—he's proud of the program he has

Seung-been "Steven" Lee developed the Stargazer computer program, which uses a patient's DNA profile to determine the correct dosage of painkiller he or she should receive.

developed, which can help doctors choose the most appropriate amount of painkiller to give patients.

Called Stargazer, the program can translate a person's DNA sequence information into a prediction of that individual's responsiveness to various drugs. The program allows doctors to prescribe drugs more safely and effectively because they can follow his program's guidance to make better drug choices and find more accurate dosing.

Codeine is a widely used painkiller, but a patient can actually die from taking a normal dose if he or she has a certain type of DNA sequence.

"There have been numerous cases where people actually died because doctors did not know whether their patients were sensitive to codeine," he says. "Conversely, one could also have a certain DNA type that makes him or her not responsive to codeine at all."

For the Stargazer program to work, a patient's DNA sequence information must be acquired. To do this, clinicians use a DNA sequencer, a scientific instrument that determines the precise order of nucleotides within a DNA molecule from a blood sample.

The Stargazer program only investigates certain segments of DNA (known as "genes") that are involved in drug metabolism. Human DNA is very long and not all sections are useful for predicting drug metabolism. Stargazer uses many complex algorithms to accurately detect all types of mutations so that nothing is missed.

Because the input DNA sequence comes in the form of an electronic file, Stargazer is programmed so that it knows how to import DNA sequence information from the given input file.

"We performed rigorous testing to validate Stargazer's performance, and its accuracy was at least 99.0%," says Lee.

Lee recommends that anyone interested in health care at least familiarize himself or herself with programming. "The ability to determine whether or not some task can be done with programming is becoming increasingly important," he says. "Once you realize a problem can be solved with programming, you can always find a person to implement your solution for you even if you do not know the computer language."

CHAPTER FIVE

ROBOTICS AND BEYOND

Across the globe, robotic surgery is on the rise, but it does not mean an army of R2-D2-like characters from the *Star Wars* movies will be coming at patients with scalpels. With this technology, surgeons sit behind computer consoles and direct robotic arms to perform procedures. By the year 2021, one in three surgeries in the United States is expected to be performed with robotic systems, according to *Fortune* magazine.

Since gaining approval from the Food and Drug Administration in 2000, the company Intuitive Surgical has dominated the robotic surgery field with its da Vinci Surgical System. Da Vinci helps perform laparoscopic surgery, a technique involving small incisions and long pencil-like instruments that move as commanded. Often patients prefer this approach over standard surgery because it offers less wear and tear on the body. Recovery times can be faster when incisions are smaller.

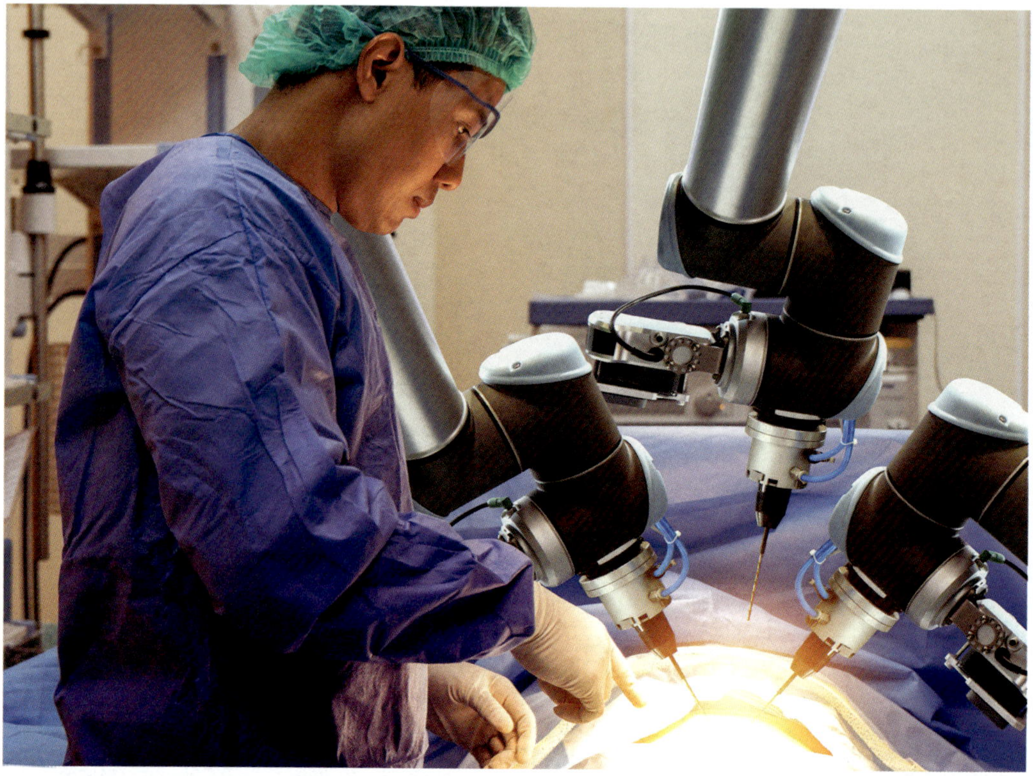

To perform precise and delicate operations, surgeons may rely on the computer and software technology of robotic-assisted surgical devices.

Robotic surgery can fix a hernia (when an organ pushes through an opening in the muscle or tissue that holds it in place) or create a gastric bypass, which modifies the stomach to hold less food so a patient can lose weight. It's commonly used for hysterectomies (removal of all or part of the uterus) and the majority of prostate removals.

The robotic controls are designed to give greater dexterity, control, and precision. A tiny 3D camera relays images to a screen giving the surgeon a better view from inside the body. The equipment has provided the means to record instructive motion and video data as well.

There are some downsides. Robotic surgery typically costs much more than a regular operation, and mishaps have occurred that have injured patients (although this can happen during normal surgery as well). Some surgeons say that setting up the equipment takes too much time.

These million-dollar machines operate with precision because of the coding developed by software engineers at medical technology firms. A 2017 article published by the medical industry employment firm the Mullings Group found that many individuals from the gaming industry were finding work coding for surgical robotics because of the similarities among both industries. The robotics team at UCLA also compares operating robotic surgical equipment to playing a video game. A surgeon guides the computerized instruments, which perform precise operations inside a patient's body exactly as instructed.

WHAT ROBOTICS PROS NEED TO KNOW

Coding for this equipment is challenging—a software designer must program the robot's every motion down to the tiniest detail or the results can be potentially life-threatening. Though the top computer languages in robotics include C and C++, Python, and Java, those

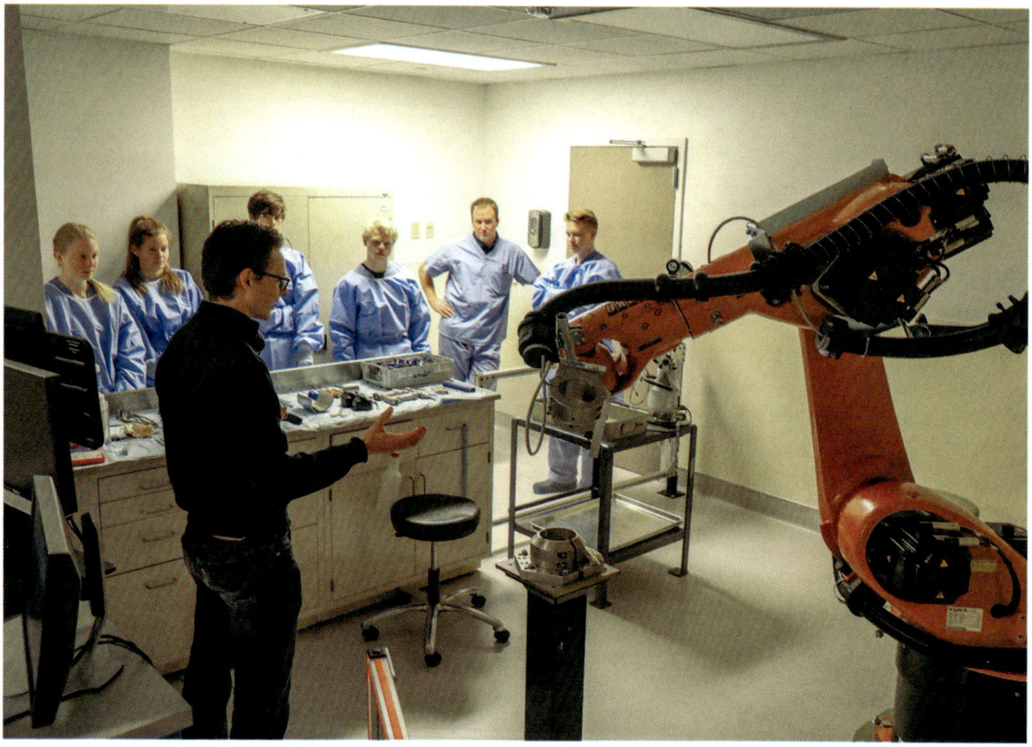

Robotics engineer Alex Brady explains to students how an old car manufacturing robot has been reprogrammed to perform rotator cuff surgery.

who delve deeper into this field may explore MATLAB, Assembly, Hardware Description Languages, LISP, Industrial Robot Languages, and BASIC/Pascal.

For those pursuing a career in robotics, many colleges and universities offer degrees in robotics, including the University of Massachusetts-Amherst, University of Minnesota, University of Tennessee-Knoxville, University of Pennsylvania, and the Massachusetts Institute of Technology (MIT). UC

Berkeley has a dedicated Center for Automation and Learning for Medical Robotics where students learn to improve robots and devices for medicine and surgery. In 2013, a team of researchers at the University of California at Berkeley published research on the application of an algorithm for automated suturing performed by robots.

The Bureau of Labor Statistics reports that demand for robotics professionals is expected to grow over the next ten years.

WILL ROBOTS REPLACE HUMANS?

So far, robots have been assisting surgeons but not putting them out of work. Jacob Rosen, associate professor of computer engineering at the University of California in Santa Cruz, said in an interview with *Scientific American* magazine that it would be difficult for a computer program to adjust to the way a patient's skin, internal organs, and tissue change shape and move during surgery. Humans are needed to make critical decisions during the surgery process.

With that said, programmers and robotics engineers have been stepping into the arena of fully automated surgery. In 2016, the Children's National Health System in Washington, DC, used the Smart Tissue Autonomous Robot (STAR) to accurately repair pigs' bowels without any human assistance. In tests so far, outcomes have been equal to that of a skilled surgeon. The idea is to not put surgeons out of work. By automating repetitive surgical subtasks, such as suturing and cutting, fatigue and procedure times can be reduced.

WHEN MACHINES START LEARNING

A new wave of automated surgery relies on artificial intelligence and data gathered from robotic systems. At Johns Hopkins University, researchers have been recording robot-assisted surgeries. Their goal is to collect large amounts of data, known as "big data," regarding all the features of a surgery—such as techniques used and movements made. With big data, they can write better algorithms so surgical equipment can respond to more possible scenarios. On the Johns Hopkins University website, Greg Hager, professor of computer science and director of the Malone Center for Engineering in Healthcare, says, "That's the power of big data. I suspect once you've seen a few million people, you've probably seen 99.99 percent of the variants you're going to run into."

Based on data, surgical robots may be able to "learn." Machine learning is a field of computer science that uses computer systems to perform functions without being specifically programmed. The computer "learns" from data it is given or acquires. It is part of an overall concept called artificial intelligence, or AI, which is about programming machines to perform complex jobs.

Programmers are coming up with algorithms based on the function and structure of the brain

START LEARNING ROBOTICS

Robotics education is sweeping the country. A growing number of high schools run their own robotics clubs, in which students get hands-on experience building and programming their creations. Young robotics enthusiasts have been gathering at contests such as FIRST Robotics Competition and VEX Robotics World Championship. The Technology Student Association provides helpful resources for those wanting to delve deeper into the subject.

Those who are serious about developing this type of tech may look into higher-education institutions that offer precollege summer technology programs. Carnegie Mellon Robotics Academy offers a simple-to-learn Robotics Education Curriculum that teaches students who know nothing about robotics to eventually program advanced behaviors.

called artificial neural networks. This cutting-edge concept is part of "deep learning," a machine learning technique that teaches computers to learn by example. Students interested in these advanced areas are advised to have a knowledge of linear algebra, calculus, and statistics. There are courses available online, such as Practical Deep Learning for

Coders, that can ease a programmer into this new field.

ADVANCES FOR ARTIFICIAL LIMBS

Robotics is also helping patients who have lost limbs. Advanced prosthetics have begun tapping into brain signals to provide amputees with remarkable new levels of control. For example, the Prosthetics Department at Johns Hopkins is creating an artificial limb that works off of a person's nervous system. The goal is to restore near-natural motor function and senses to people who have lost a limb. Advanced prosthetics move because of interactions among actuators (mechanisms by which control systems act), sensors, microprocessors, and embedded control software. Limb inventors envision their products using specific design software.

In the medical world, virtual reality is another type of technology that is being used for therapy, offering another opportunity for coders to develop innovative products that can improve and save lives.

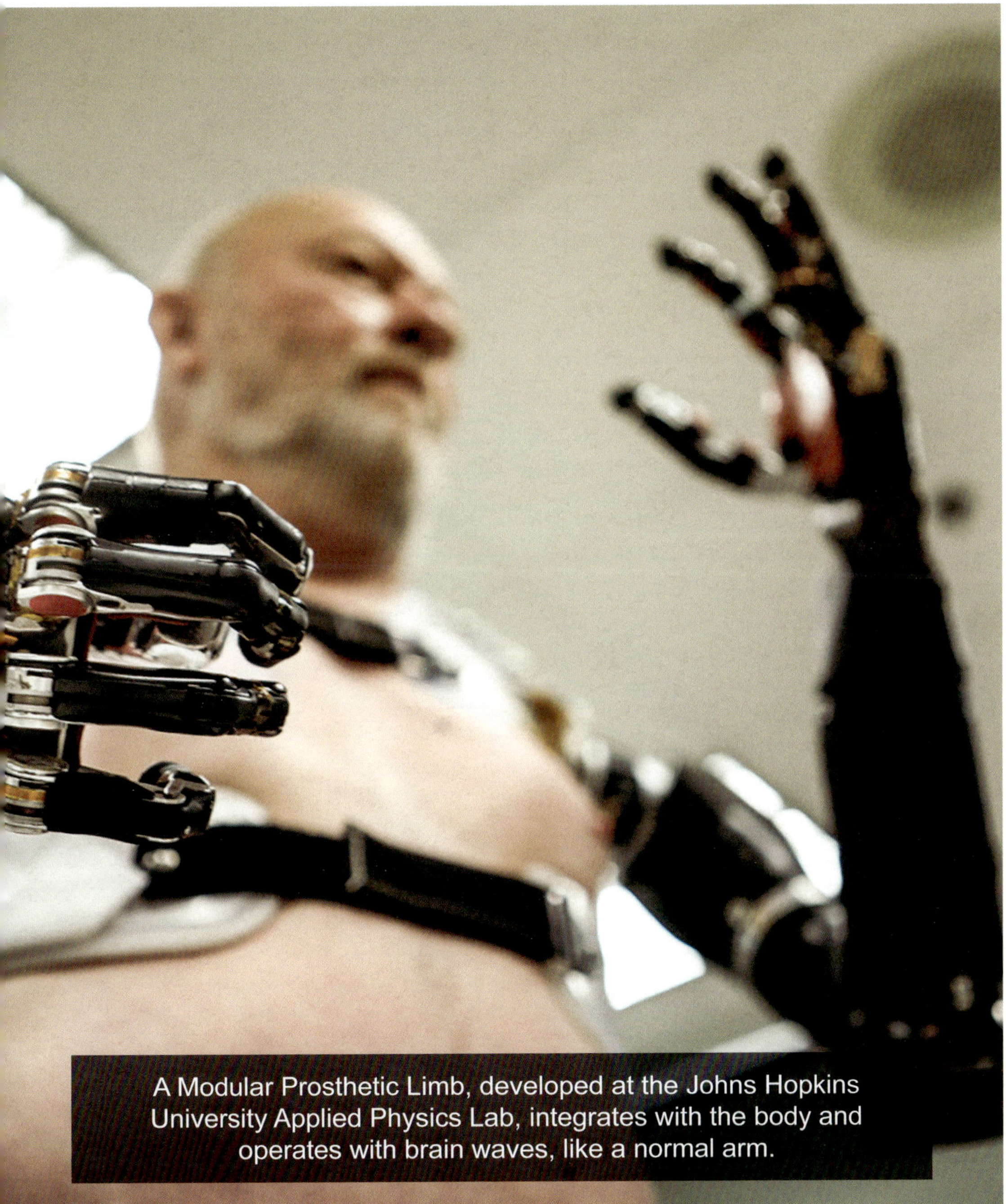

A Modular Prosthetic Limb, developed at the Johns Hopkins University Applied Physics Lab, integrates with the body and operates with brain waves, like a normal arm.

Beyond robots, AI is changing other medical equipment as well. Recently, medical technology firm Arterys introduced a medical imaging platform that can help doctors diagnose heart problems. The platform is cloud based, meaning that it doesn't have to be downloaded. It is maintained and stored on servers via the internet. The software relies on a self-teaching artificial neural network that has learned from thousands of cases—with each new heart imaging, it learns a little bit more about how the heart works. In less than a half minute, Arterys can evaluate blood flow through the heart using magnetic resonance imaging analysis—a process that would normally take medical professionals thirty minutes to an hour to perform.

CHAPTER SIX

COMPUTING TO FIND THE CURE

As doctors look for the cure for cancer and other diseases, they rely on a knowledge of medicine, biology, and chemistry. Computer programming, however, may also open the door to finding answers. Microchips are just as important as microscopes when it comes to research. Instead of test tubes, coders rely on algorithms to come up with health care solutions.

Software developers are creating systems to sort through research data to help oncologists come up with individualized treatments for cancer patients. Genetics researchers write complex computer codes to sift through mountains of data. Their goal is to pinpoint the specific genes that cause diseases or to discover the specific treatment that will work best for each person.

Technology firm NVDIA sponsors the Compute the Cure program, which provides grants for research centered on computation as the path toward a

MIT professors Tommi Jaakkola (*left*) and Regina Barzilay teach machine learning, a science of programming computers to "learn" and respond based on taking in increasing amounts of data.

cancer cure. In 2017, investigators from San Diego's Ludwig Cancer Research Institute and the University of Toronto won $200,000 from NVDIA to use deep learning to examine large data files on DNA sequencing. Their goal was to determine which mutations turn healthy cells into malignant tumors and to predict how those cells evolve.

USING ARTIFICIAL INTELLIGENCE TO SPOT DISEASE

At MIT, computer scientists developed a model to distinguish types of lymphoma. Using archived pathology reports, they wrote a program that matched types of test results to certain types of lymphoma. Another group of investigators at MIT, led by Professor Regina Barzilay, has been taking the knowledge of artificial intelligence and machine learning to come up with better methods for cancer diagnosis and treatment. Doctors can spot cancer from mammograms when a tumor starts to grow. But the complex images presented in a mammogram may hold biological clues about potential cancer prior to that. For example, Barzilay believes the right software could scour through millions of mammograms and find signs that are common to breast cancer development.

When diagnosing with these AI systems, the more information that is input, the smarter and more accurate the software becomes. A research group at Mount Sinai Hospital in New York City made a program called Deep Patient that reviewed data on more than seven hundred thousand patients. By looking for patterns and common characteristics, the program became a fairly reliable predictor for who might later get a specific illness, such as liver cancer. Doctors have found that Deep Patient had a high accuracy rate when it came to predicting schizophrenia.

A DOCTOR'S RESEARCH VIA APPS

Dr. E. Kevin Hall, medical director of the Pediatric Heart Failure and Cardiomyopathy Program at Yale University School of Medicine, has been using code to do his own remote research. Since he was a young

YOUR TOOTHBRUSH IS EXAMINING YOU

Scientists are working with a type of artificial intelligence research to directly help consumers. Technology firm Philips has partnered with biotechnology company PathAI to explore ways to acquire and analyze consumer information through personal devices. For example, sensor devices in toothbrushes and wearables could transmit data to a central computer that compiles all the details. Again, based on ever-growing mountains of information, a computer program may be able to pinpoint those individuals who may be in danger of getting a cavity—all from a transmission from their toothbrushes.

boy, he's had an interest in coding and computer science. He even built his own personal computers. Today, he deals with a lot of young children who have heart defects, but he has been frustrated that he doesn't get enough time with patients to gather more valuable information. When he discovered Apple's software platform ResearchKit ("A software framework for apps that let medical researchers gather robust and meaningful data," according to Apple), he realized that he could create an app that would make a smartphone into a valuable research tool.

Using ResearchKit's open-source code, he created a clinical study to assess quality of life of patients who may be at risk of developing cardiomyopathy, a

Jeff Williams, senior vice president of operations at Apple, introduces ResearchKit, software that helps medical researchers create iPhone apps to gather data and conduct research.

heart muscle abnormality. One of his challenges was coding a parental consent document that was needed so children under the age of eighteen could send in health information through the app. In the end, Hall hopes that the data collected through the app will ultimately lead to improved medical care as doctors gain a better understanding of the symptoms and risks young heart patients face.

In addition to Philips, other big tech companies, such as IBM, Alphabet, and Microsoft, are immersed in the world of AI research. Microsoft has introduced the cloud-based Bio Model Analyzer that allows researchers to compare the normal workings of healthy cells to the abnormal processes in diseased cells. The tool has been helpful in identifying which patients will develop a resistance to a drug therapy.

PROGRESS FOR PUBLIC HEALTH

In the health care field, scientists compile and interpret information from computer databases from around the world. These professionals may predict trends in illness or identify successful treatments. They rely on computer programs such as statistical software applications most commonly employed for data analysis in health services research.

Another branch of health care research is epidemiology. Epidemiologists are public health professionals who investigate patterns and causes of disease and injury in humans, according to the BLS. Through research, health policy, and community

PROGRAMMING HUMAN CELLS

Can a living cell ever be made into a tiny, tiny computer? Biologists at Microsoft, MIT, Stanford, and other organizations think so. They have been looking into ways to transform cells into living computers that can be programmed to treat cancer and other diseases. Through genetic engineering, they are looking for ways to build circuits out of DNA and proteins. Scientists believe that a cell might be able to be programmed to detect cancer—then if detected, that cell might produce a drug that could fight the cancer. Building cellular systems such as this may be in the experimental stages now, but the future of health care may depend on this novel concept. The ability to make technology small is at the foundation of nanotechnology, a science devoted to the manipulation of matter on an atomic, molecular, and supramolecular scale. The Max Planck Institute, a research institute, for instance, has been working on microsized robots that can swim through the bloodstream and deliver drugs to targeted locations.

education, these professionals try to lower the risk of negative health outcomes. They often work for state and local governments in health departments. Hospitals, colleges, and universities may also hire epidemiologists. The federal government's Centers for

Disease Control and Prevention (CDC) also depends on their research and expertise.

One of their specialties is to gather and evaluate demographic data to identify who is at the highest risk for a certain disease. They often use a software package called the Statistical Analysis System. Statistics is the science of collecting, reviewing, and interpreting vast amounts of data to find underlying patterns and trends—it's really the precursor to the big data collection that helps with AI. Powerful computers and advanced algorithms allow epidemiologists to run multiple permutations of their calculations.

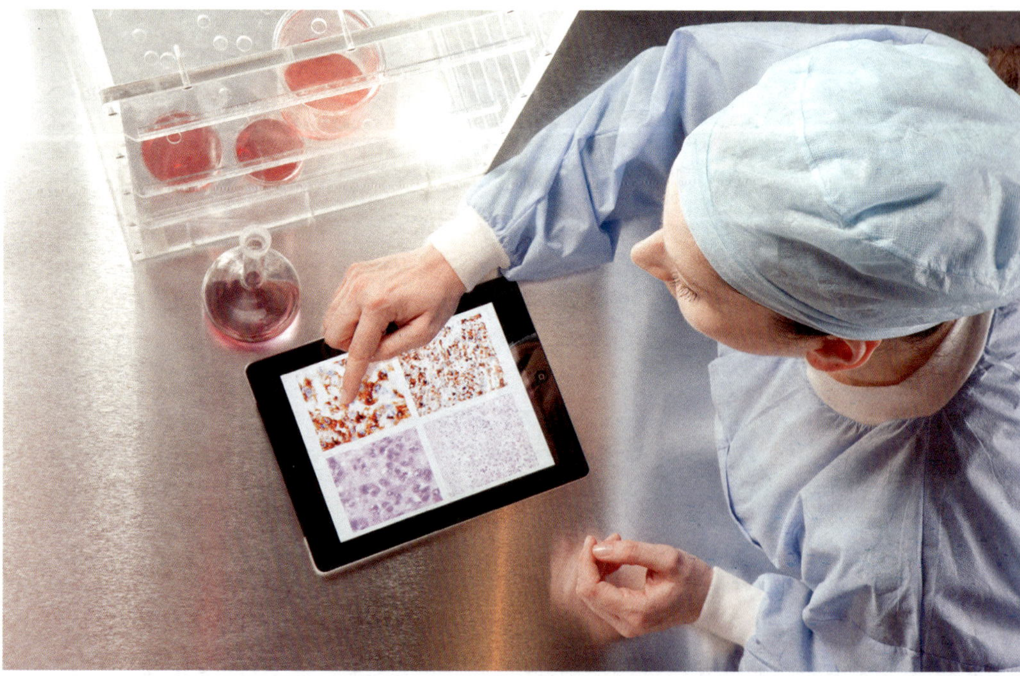

Epidemiologists are public health scientists who investigate the disease patterns and the cause of outbreaks, using statistical software and other computer-based analyses.

The Bureau of Labor Statistics reports that jobs for epidemiologists are expected to grow 9 percent from 2016 to 2026. Epidemiologists need at least a master's degree from an accredited college or university, according to the BLS. Most epidemiologists have a master's degree in public health (MPH) or a related field, while some have gone on to finish a doctoral degree in epidemiology or medicine.

In the pharmaceutical industry, statistical programmers are key players, analyzing collected data that will help in the development of new medications. Programming for statistical analysis also provides the skills that are transferable to a career in AI and big data.

CHAPTER SEVEN

PATIENT POWER THROUGH TECHNOLOGY

Patients have become more empowered about their health as technology has improved communication and spread health care knowledge. Computer programming has also brought better connections between health care providers and those for whom they care.

The web has been the primary driver for boosting consumer education on all matters related to health. The internet is an encyclopedic information source. For those who write code, opportunities are far reaching because so many different organizations and businesses need programming expertise that is specifically web related.

Some programming jobs related to health care may require a more sophisticated knowledge of artificial intelligence, statistics, and medical concepts, but web developers can generally rely on a standard set of programming skills. In the workplace, web developers are in high demand, with employment projected to

Web developers have created many medical information sites to provide consumers with helpful health advice and news, though they are not designed to replace a doctor's expertise.

grow 15 percent from 2016 to 2026. Educational requirements for web development positions can vary from a high school diploma to a bachelor's degree—it all depends on the type of work being performed. No matter the job, web development requires both programming and graphic design knowledge.

LEARNING THE LANGUAGE OF THE WEB

In the world of web design, there are components that consumers view on the "front end," via their computer screens, and there are functions and information accessed on the "back end," or on servers. The back end is the real brainpower behind what individuals see on their screens.

Programmers who bring a website to life on the front end must learn about Hypertext Markup Language (HTML), Cascading Style Sheets (CSS), and JavaScript. Together, these form the mighty triad of coding around which all websites are built. HTML allows a person to design a web page so it can present text, images, and links to other web pages, videos, interactive forms, and more. CSS are instructions that "style" web pages, defining how they should look in terms of fonts and colors. These sheets tell the computer or mobile browser how content should look to the user. CSS define layout, position, alignment, height, width, typefaces, borders, etc. While HTML and CSS are used to create the presentation of a web page, JavaScript brings functionality. JavaScript implements interactive and dynamic features such as animations, video, games, and scrolling abilities.

Computer users see the results of programming on their graphical user interface (GUI), the visual display on a computer screen that allows the user to interact with the web page. The GUI includes graphical elements, such as windows, icons, and buttons.

LISTENING TO CUSTOMER NEEDS

Epic Systems is one of America's leading medical record software providers. Judy Faulkner developed its software using Massachusetts General Hospital Utility Multi-Programming System (MUMPS)—a code developed in the late 1960s. She started the company in 1979 with just three employees in a Wisconsin basement. She launched the firm with a $70,000 loan borrowed against the value of her house. Now, the Epic workforce tops 9,400 employees, and Faulkner has a net worth of about $3.7 billion.

Faulkner started out as a math major in college and branched out to computer science in graduate school. In an interview in *Forbes*, Faulkner said that a key to being a successful software company has been listening to customers. "We try to listen to our users and develop products they need," she said. "Programmers who are new to an application visit six to eight customers the first year to learn how the users do their jobs." Those considering a programming career can take inspiration from Faulkner. Why did she enter the field? Because she thought programming was fun!

On the back end, where a great deal of the work of the web happens, developers typically depend on the languages PHP, Java, Python, Ruby, or SQL. Through coding, a pharmacy may set up an online form for refilling prescriptions or a doctor's office may present a survey to rate the quality of its services.

Learning web languages can be a good place to begin programming because students can try out the tools on their home computers and take online tutorials for guidance. Honing web programming skills can open doors and help a candidate advance in any segment of the health care industry.

HEALTH INFORMATION SITES

The internet can help educate people in almost every health subject through thousands of different websites. For the latest news, consumers may turn to sites such as WebMD, HealthDay, and Everyday Health, or scores of blogs that discuss health matters. Consumers can choose from a vast selection of nutrition, diet, and exercise advice as well.

The federal government's National Library of Medicine offers the site MedlinePlus, which defines all sorts of medical terms and presents information on health conditions and wellness issues. The Food and Drug Administration provides the latest reports on medications. Nonprofit organizations such as the American Cancer Society, American Heart Association, American Diabetes Association, National Institute of Mental Health, and Leukemia and Lymphoma Society maintain web pages filled with practical guidance. The public can also access vital articles posted by hospitals, clinics, and research

Individuals can find many sites designed to assist with health issues. Healthcare Magic, for example, provides online answers to medical questions for a fee.

groups, such as the Mayo Clinic, Memorial Sloan Kettering Cancer Center, and the University of Texas MD Anderson Cancer Center.

The handiwork of coders can be seen in online forums that let patients discuss issues with a large audience. For example, HealthBoards connects people who may have similar illnesses and ailments, which can provide comfort and shared resources. On a higher programming level, coders have constructed search engines expressly for questions regarding well-being, such as Healthline, MedHunt, and Omni Medical Search. Consumers can also access medical-related podcasts and videocasts.

PERSONAL CARE TOOLS

Health insurance companies and doctor's offices have been setting up computer systems that allow patients to view records and manage their health care from home. These sites let patients change doctors, update contact information, request ID cards, get health care reminders on services needed, view visit history, and make payments. Mobile phone apps can also let consumers tap into their records.

In January 2018, Apple updated its Health app with a feature that lets customers see their medical records right on their iPhones. Johns Hopkins Medicine, Cedars-Sinai, Penn Medicine, and other participating hospitals and clinics are making the tool available to their patients. In a press release, the company said that software experts designed the app

Personal care has reached a whole new level with apps that let consumers instantly check medical records and gadgets that monitor vital signs and provide other health data.

so "consumers will have medical information from various institutions organized into one view covering allergies, conditions, immunizations, lab results, medications, procedures and vitals. Customers receive notifications when their data is updated. Health record data is encrypted and protected with the user's iPhone passcode." Software that keeps the patient more engaged in his or her care helps relieve anxiety and promotes better decision making.

GLOSSARY

algorithm A step-by-step process or calculation for solving a problem.

anesthesia A drug or combination of drugs intended to block pain before surgery.

calculus A division of mathematics that mostly focuses on rates of change.

console A terminal attached to a computer.

CT (computed tomography) A technology that produces a three-dimensional image of a body structure.

database management The organization and maintenance of information collected in a computer program.

debug The process of finding and fixing errors in software or hardware.

electrocardiogram A visual representation of a patient's heartbeat created by electrocardiography.

electroencephalography The measuring and recording of the brain's electrical activity in different areas.

epidemiologist A doctor who specializes in the patterns of diseases that spread among people.

informatics Also called information science, this is the science of processing data for storage and retrieval.

laparoscopic surgery Also known as keyhole surgery, a modern surgical technique performed through small incisions.

microprocessor Also known as a logic chip, a computer processor contained on an integrated-circuit chip.

MRI (magnetic resonance imaging) A method of obtaining internal images of living things using a magnetic field and radio waves.

neurology A branch of science that deals with nerves and the nervous system.

oxygenation The process of adding oxygen to a substance or system.

statistics The science of gathering and evaluating large quantities of numerical information.

wearables Electronics that can be worn on the body.

Association of Information Technology Professionals (AITP)
3500 Lacey Road, Suite 100
Downers Grove, IL 60515
(866) 835-8020
Website: https://www.aitp.org
This worldwide society of professionals in information technology offers career training, scholarships, news, and social networking opportunities.

Canada Learning Code
129 Spadina Avenue
Toronto, ON M5V 2L3
Canada
(647) 715-4555
Website: http://www.canadalearningcode.ca
This organization has a mission to provide digital skills to all Canadians.

Canadian Advanced Technology Alliance (CATA)
207 Bank Street, Suite 416
Ottawa, ON K2P 2N2
Canada
(613) 236-6550
Website: http://www.cata.ca
The largest high-tech association in Canada, CATA is a comprehensive resource of the latest high-tech news in Canada.

Canada's Association of I.T. Professionals (CIPS)
1375 Southdown Road
Unit 16 - Suite 802
Mississauga, ON L5J 2Z1
Canada
(905) 602-1370
Website: http://www.cips.ca
This association offers networking opportunities, certification, and accreditation in information technology.

Code.org
1501 4th Avenue
Seattle, WA 98101
Website: http://www.code.org
This nonprofit is dedicated to expanding access to computer science in schools and increasing participation by women and underrepresented minorities. Its vision is that every student in every school should have the opportunity to learn computer science.

TryComputing.org
501 Hoes Lane
Piscataway, NJ 08854-4141
(732) 981-0060
Website: http://www.trycomputing.org
This site from the Institute of Electrical and Electronics Engineers features competitions, events, internships, and research programs for young people. Also find out about career opportunities and colleges with computer programming courses.

FOR FURTHER READING

Bedell, Jane. *So, You Want to Be a Coder?* New York, NY: Alladin/Simon & Schuster, 2016.

Ceceri, Kathy. *Robotics: Discover the Science and Technology of the Future with 20 Projects.* White River Junction, VT: Nomad Press, 2012.

Keogh, Jim. *Health Informatics Demystified*. New York, NY: McGraw-Hill Professional, 2014.

MacManus, Richard. *Health Trackers: How Technology Is Helping Us Monitor and Improve Our Health*. Boulder, CO: Rowman & Littlefield, 2015.

Swanson, Jennifer. *Everything Robotics: All the Photos, Facts, and Fun to Make You Race for Robots* (National Geographic Kids). Washington, DC: National Geographic Children's Books, 2016.

Vanden-Heuvel, John C. *Web Design for Kids*. New York, NY: Little Bee Books, 2016.

Wainewright, Max. *How to Code: A Step-by-Step Guide to Computer Coding*. Asheville, NC: Sterling Children's Books, 2016.

Woodcock, Jon, and Kiki Prottsman. *Star Wars Coding Projects*. New York, NY: DK Publishing, 2017.

Woodcock, Jon, and Steve Setford. *DK Workbooks: Coding in Scratch: Games Workbook*. New York, NY: DK Publishing, 2016.

BIBLIOGRAPHY

Apple Press. "Apple announces effortless solution bringing health records to iPhone." January 24, 2018. https://www.apple.com/newsroom/2018/01/apple-announces-effortless-solution-bringing-health-records-to-iPhone.

Becker's Health & CIO Review. "10 Technologies to Keep Hospitals Competitive." January 17, 2012. https://www.beckershospitalreview.com/healthcare-information-technology/10-technologies-to-keep-hospitals-competitive.html.

Bond, Allison. "Why Do Doctors Still Use Pagers?" February 12, 2016. http://www.slate.com/articles/health_and_science/medical_examiner/2016/02/why_do_doctors_still_use_pagers.html.

Casimir, Patrick. "Health Informatics, a Fast-Growing Field and a Crucial Skill-Set." Theoretically Speaking: The Official Blog of HealthEconomics.com, June 2015. http://www.healtheconomics.com/blog/2015/06/health-informatics-fast-growing-field-crucial-skill-set.

David, Solomon. "Students Across Nation Join Together to Build Wearable Fitness Trackers." SportTechie, October 2, 2017. https://www.sporttechie.com/students-build-wearable-fitness-trackers.

Fierce Healthcare. "Family Physicians Provide Insight on Consumer Health Technology." January 12, 2015. https://www.fiercehealthcare.com/it/family-physicians-provide-insights-consumer-health-technology.

Graham, Paul. "Knuth: Computer Programming as an Art." PaulGraham.com, December 1974. http://www.paulgraham.com/knuth.html.

Greenemeier, Larry. "Robotic Surgery Opens Up." *Scientific American*, February 11, 2014. https://www.scientificamerican.com/article/robotic-surgery-opens-up.

Heathman, Amelia. "Microsoft wants to 'solve' cancer in the next 10 years using AI." *Wired*, September 20, 2016. http://www.wired.co.uk/article/microsoft-solve-cancer-computer-science.

Kim, Michelle. "New Technologies Bring Surgery into the World of Big Data." Johns Hopkins Medicine, January 25, 2016. https://biomedicalodyssey.blogs.hopkinsmedicine.org/2016/01/new-technologies-bring-surgery-into-the-world-of-big-data.

Kubben, Pieter. "Why physicians might want to learn computer programming." *Surgical Neurology International*, March 22, 2013. https://www.ncbi.nlm.nih.gov/pmc/articles/PMC3622380.

Lamar, Elise. "New computer program detects cancer by blood sampling." UCLA Research Alert, March 28, 2017. http://newsroom.ucla.edu/releases/ucla-researchers-devise-computer-program-to-detect-and-localize-cancer-by-blood-sampling.

Mesko, Bertalan. "10 Ways Technology Is Changing Healthcare." MedicalFuturist.com. Retrieved March 5, 2018. http://medicalfuturist.com/ten-ways-technology-changing-healthcare.

Motti, Judy. "Yale's E. Kevin Hall: Digital health tools must facilitate a shared dialogue." Fierce Healthcare, July 5, 2016. https://www

.fiercehealthcare.com/mobile/fmh-feature-profile-yale-s-kevin-hall-offers-insight-researchkit-state-mhealth-tech.

Moukheiber, Zina. "An Interview with the Most Powerful Woman in Healthcare." *Forbes*, May 15, 2013. https://www.forbes.com/sites/zinamoukheiber/2013/05/15/a-chat-with-epic-systems-ceo-judy-faulkner/#7d6805956c13.

Restuccia, Dan. "Code This Software, STAT: Programming Skills in Medicine." BurningGlass Technologies, June 23, 2016. https://www.burningglass.com/blog/code-this-software-stat-programming-skills-in-medicine.

SAS: Analytics, Business Intelligence and Data Management. "Statistical Analysis." Retrieved March 5, 2018. https://www.sas.com/en_us/insights/analytics/statistical-analysis.html.

Science Daily. "System unveiled for regulating anesthesia via computer." February 18, 2010. https://www.sciencedaily.com/releases/2010/02/100218092854.htm.

Techwalla. "Role of Computers in Medical Lab Technology." Retrieved March 5, 2018. https://www.techwalla.com/articles/role-of-computers-in-medical-lab-technology.

Tirrell, Meg. "From coding to cancer: How AI is changing medicine." CNBC, May 11, 2017. https://www.cnbc.com/2017/05/11/from-coding-to-cancer-how-ai-is-changing-medicine.html.

INDEX

ABOUT THE AUTHOR

Don Rauf is the author of numerous nonfiction books, including *Powering Up a Career in Internet Security, Computer Game Designer, Schwinn: The Best Present Ever, Killer Lipstick and Other Spy Gadgets,* and *American Inventions*. He lives in Seattle with his wife, Monique, and son, Leo.

PHOTO CREDITS

Cover JGI/Tom Grill/Blend Images/Getty Images; back cover and pp. 4–5 (background) nadla/E+/Getty Images; p. 5 © iStockphoto.com/AnthonyRosenberg; pp. 7, 14, 23, 32, 41, 51, 60 janews/Shutterstock.com; p. 8 AleksandarNakic/E+/Getty Images; p. 9 BEST-BACKGROUNDS/Shutterstock.com; p. 12 Gary Burchell/DigitalVision/Getty Images; p. 15 Ariel Skelley/Digital Vision/Getty Images; p. 17 Portra/E+/Getty Images; p. 21 Casimiro PT/Shutterstock.com; pp. 24–25 Martin Barraud/OJO Images/Getty Images; p. 27 Monty Rakusen/Cultura/Getty Images; p. 29 Kris Connor/Getty Images; p. 33 Andriy Solovyov/Shutterstock.com; p. 35 Nestor Rizhniak/Shutterstock.com; p. 37 nicolas_/E+/Getty Images; p. 39 Courtesy of Steven Lee; p. 42 Zapp2Photo/Shutterstock.com; p. 44 © AP Images; pp. 48–49 Zackary Canepari/The New York Times/Redux Pictures; p. 52 Boston Globe/Getty Images; p. 55 Stephen Lam/Getty Images; p. 58 Steve McAlister/Photolibrary/Getty Images; p. 61 © iStockphoto.com/Creativeye99; p. 65 Mint/Hindustan Times/Getty Images; p. 67 blackzheep/Shutterstock.com; interior design graphic (abstract circuit) Titima Ongkantong/Shutterstock.com.

Design: Mike Moy; Layout: Nicole Russo-Duca; Photo Researcher: Karen Huang